SIMON &
SCHUSTER

THE ULTIMATE
Bushisms

THE FIRST TERM, IN HIS OWN SPECIAL WORDS

EDITED BY

Jacob Weisberg

WITH A FOREWORD BY

Mark Steel

SIMON &
SCHUSTER

★★★★★★★★★★★★★★★★★★★★★★★★★

This edition first published by Simon & Schuster UK Ltd, 2004
A Viacom Company

Copyright © Jacob Weisberg, 2004
Foreword copyright © Mark Steel, 2004
Introduction copyright © Molly Ivins, 2004

1 3 5 7 9 10 8 6 4 2

Simon & Schuster UK Ltd
Africa House
64–78 Kingsway
London WC2B 6AH

www.simonsays.co.uk

Simon & Schuster Australia
Sydney

A CIP catalogue record for this book is available from the British Library

ISBN 0-7432-6315-4

Printed and bound in Great Britain by
Mackays of Chatham plc

PHOTO CREDITS
AP/Wide World Photos: vii, 10, 24, 27, 31, 38, 41, 79, 83, 88, 96, 98.
Mike Blake/Reuters/Landov: 70, 103. Jim Bourg/Reuters/Landov:
7, 50. Larry Downing/Reuters/Landov: photo in oval at page tops,
iii, xiii, 3, 20, 35, 44, 55, 86. Brooks Kraft/Corbis: 19, 62, 82, 92.
Kevin Lamarque/Reuters/Landov: 11. Jason Reed/Reuters/Landov:
25, 54, 66, 93. Reuters/Corbis: 65. Dennis Sabangan/EPA/Landov: 15, 63.
Joseph Sohm, Chromo Sohm Inc./Corbis: vi. Shawn Thew/EPA/Landov:
16, 37, 74. Rick Wilking/Reuters/Landov: 1, 43, 75

★★★★★★★★★★★★★★★★★★★★★★★★★

Contents

Foreword by Mark Steel

BY THE SPRING OF 2004, GEORGE BUSH'S VACANT smirk made him appear more bemused than ever, a reminder of rulers in the past whose characters haven't quite matched the enormous events they were surrounded by. Tsar Nicholas the Second, on the day he was forced to fold up his ruling bodies, wrote in his diary, 'Today I went paddling in a canoe.' Even more concisely, on the day of the storming of the Bastille, King Louis XVI wrote in his diary one word – 'Nothing.' To be fair to them, at least their diary entries were, in and of themselves coherent. If Bush had been in the Tsar's position he'd probably have written 'I've always canoed in freedom, and today I paddled in no exception.'

The cause of his ever greater bemusement was that he'd done much of what he'd set out to do, but no one was reacting as they were meant to. He'd overthrown Saddam, even captured him in a hole, but instead of guaranteeing his re-election, this issue threatened him with defeat. Friends were deserting him on a daily basis. David Kay, sent to uncover Saddam's weapons, resigned asserting they didn't exist. Bush's ex-treasury secretary Paul O'Neill caused great embarrassment when he produced a book declaring the war was fought for bogus reasons. By the time the Spanish government announced it was withdrawing its troops from Iraq, it seemed like the final scenes of *Twelve Angry Men*. Bush, Rumsfeld and Blair were the last characters ignoring the evidence to defend the project, and the whole episode might end with Bush hurling a photograph to the ground and yelling 'Bloody dads, you do your best and, baah what the hell.'

In this context the incoherent ramblings so expertly documented in this book made him a figure of greater than ever fun/contempt. But this wasn't always the case. It seems a long time ago, but in the nine months after the attack on the Twin Towers, the bulk of Western politicians and the media insisted he was the ideal figure to sort out terrorism, Bin Laden and the Middle East.

Yet this was the same George Bush. I remember him

announcing he was 'Tightening the noose around Bin Laden's neck,' by 'freezing his bank account.' As if, until then, Bin Laden was merrily strolling along to the cash-point, but now if he rang up for theatre tickets he'd be told 'I'm afraid your payment hasn't been authorized Mr. Bin Laden.' And just as he was about to get his gold card as well. Maybe the next plan was to thighten the noose further by cancelling his Blockbuster video card.

Alongside the bank account strategy, Bush announced 'Let the terrorists be warned – if you stay one day after your visa has expired, you'll be arrested.' So if you're a terrorist, make sure you carry out your bombing before the visa runs out. After all, if you're caught blowing up a skyscraper you'll be in enough trouble as it is.

When he informed us that Bin Laden had sent out a fax message full of his evil intentions, virtually every media outlet published this as fact, without asking whether it was likely that Bin Laden, in the circumstances, was likely to communicate in this way. Maybe the CIA could dial 1471 and Bingo, they'd know where he was. It's only surprising that Bush didn't claim Bin Laden had sent a text message – 'It is duT of IsLM 2 rise in holy Ghad. Praise 2 LR the almiT.'

And he insisted at one stage that he could do a deal with the 'moderate Taliban'. The moderate Taliban? I suppose they're the ones that said 'Well one tower yes, but not both.'

Around this time the question arose of whether Bush had been so obsessed with Saddam, that he'd ignored warnings of a possible attack on America from Bin Laden. One of his first answers to this question was 'You know what's interesting about Washington? It's a town, unfortunately.'

By the time of the invasion of Iraq, Bush's prounouncements had moved from the nutty to the sinister. It's reported that as he was about to go on air to inform the world the invasion had begun, he clapped his hands and yelped, 'I feel good.'

By now most of the Western world was questioning Bush's strategy, to the extent that many countries witnessed their largest ever demonstrations. And the disapproval grew stronger when the weapons of mass destruction that had been the purpose of the war failed to turn up. Bush even suggested it didn't matter whether the weapons were there or not, which after all the fuss about them, was as if the Wily Coyote finally caught the Road Runner, and said 'To tell you the truth I'm not that hungry.'

As the Bush strategy began to unravel at both ends, some of those who had backed him were feeling a little

Introduction by Molly Ivins

AUSTIN—THE NOBLE AND VALIANT ARCHIVAL masterpiece that is the collected Bushisms of course owes its existence to the hundreds, even thousands by now, of volunteers who sat dumbfounded while trying to figure out "Did he just actually say that?" AND who then took that all-important step of passing the miswronger along to Jacob Weisberg for the definitive collection. This gladdens my populist heart: citizen involvement, alert Americans, guardian watchdogs of democracy. Let's have a salute to these collectors of clangers, savers of solecisms, and distraught English teachers from coast to coast.

Like Weisberg, I first began collecting Bushisms under Bush the Elder, whose daffy way with words bemused everyone who ever had to take notes on him. The Elder would leap into a sentence headfirst, swimming valiantly through clause after clause, his head barely above water, with neither subject nor predicate in sight, and at last arrive exhausted at a randomly placed period. By the time he got through, we in the press often had no idea what he had just said, nor had he. A friend of mine interviewed the Elder when he first ran for the House of Representatives in 1966. After spending a day watching his campaign, she complimented him on the active corps of women volunteers he had working for him. "Aren't they great?" he said, beaming. "I call them the Beaver Patrol!"

W., in my opinion, does not rival his daddy for sheer daffiness of effect: with W., you can mostly tell what he meant to say even when he goes astray, as he often does. During his years as governor, W. had the great advantage of being surrounded by other Texas politicians, who are famous as a group for mangling the language. Here in the Great State we have many individual contenders who can outdo Bush in slaughtering syntax on any given Sunday. (A teacher once approached the notoriously inarticulate Speaker of the Texas House Gib Lewis—his only native language is Gibberish—to complain about his syntax, causing the Speaker to reply in genuine indignation. "Sin tax? Lady, I'm against all taxes!") However, as the years wore on at the old state capitol, even veterans came to admire Bush's ability to misinterprefy word program-related activities. Some of his worst verbological confusions start with an initial mistake, and then, because something in there didn't sound quite right to him, he sets out to clearify it, often with horrendous definitional misconsequences.

Our peerless leader in the Bushism field, Jacob Weisberg, has spent years trying to define and categorize our only President's misspeechifiers. Consider the awesome nature of the task: like the early naturalists, he had first to define vegetable, animal, or mineral, then to sort these misshapen lumps of English into kingdom, phylum, class, order, family, genus, and species.

Forgive me if I am presumptuous, but I would like to suggest a few additional categories, in which there is no grammatical misadventure—or neologism, spoonerism, or malapropism—but a truly original flight of wrongitude. This may come closer to some well-known errors of logic such as syllogism, sophistry, arguments *ad hominem*, arguments *ad captandum*, and arguments *add one too many*. One of my favorites in this *je ne sais quoi* school of logic is the following post–9/11 gem: "We need to counter the shock waves of the evildoer by having individual rate cuts accelerated, and by thinking about tax rebates."

Think about it: "Counter the shock waves of the evil-doer [some son of a bitch just blew up two thousand Americans] . . . by thinking about tax rebates." I believe this is in a kingdom unto itself. Then there is a common George W. rhetorical ploy, the ringing statement of the obvious, as in "I don't do nuance." Or "Our nation must come together to unite." And the ringing redundanta-mentality of the obvious, as in, "Home is important. It's important to have a home." Or "The thing that's impor-tant for me is to remember what's the most important thing." Sometimes you get the rare triple in this cate-gory, as in, "There's nothing more deep than recogniz-ing Israel's right to exist: That's the most deep thought of all: I can't think of anything more deep than that." The late Sam Attlesey of *The Dallas Morning News*, one of Texas' best political writers, was a connoisseur of Bushisms, and one of our favorite memories of Sam was the sight of his long, thin figure folded up with glee while tears of laughter ran down his cheeks as George W. tried to dig himself out of yet another rapidly collapsing sentence.

I leave it to the fearless Weisberg to continue the difficult and possibly endless task of classification. For myself, I like to take the occasional tour d'horizon on matters both foreign and domestic in George W.'s very

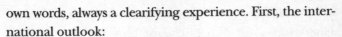

own words, always a clarifying experience. First, the international outlook:

"This foreign policy stuff is a little frustrating, whether in French or in English or in Mexican. This is a world that is much more uncertain than the past. In the past, we were certain, were certain it was us versus the Russians in the past. We were certain, and therefore we had huge nuclear arsenals aimed at each other to keep the peace. . . . You see, even though it's an uncertain world, we're certain of some things. We're certain that even though the 'evil empire' may have passed, evil still remains. We're certain there are people that can't stand what America stands for. We're certain there are madmen in this world, and there's terror, and there's missiles and I'm certain of this too: I'm certain to maintain the peace, we better have a military of high morale, and I'm certain under this administration, morale in the military is dangerously low.

"For a century and a half now America and Japan have formed one of the great and enduring alliances of modern times.

"I understand that unrest in the Middle East creates unrest throughout the region. My administration has been calling upon all the leaders in the—in the Middle East to do everything they can to stop the violence, to tell the different parties involved that peace will never happen.

"I met recently with the finance minister of the Palestinian Authority and was very impressed by his grasp of finances.

"The queen of England was neat.

"Tony Blair? We both use Colgate toothpaste.

"The Grecians, the Timorisans, and the Kosovians can all be shipped to the country of Africa.

"Russia is no longer our enemy and therefore we shouldn't be locked into a Cold War mentality that says we keep the peace by blowing each other up. In my attitude, that's old, that's tired, that's stale.

"The war on terror involves Saddam Hussein because of the nature of Saddam Hussein, the history of Saddam Hussein, and his willingness to terrorize himself.

"I think war is a dangerous place. Iran would be dangerous if they have a nuclear weapon.

"My answer is bring them on. At the same time that has to be at a level commiserate with keeping the peace."

Meanwhile, on the home front, we get the following report from the only president we've got:

"Here in the homeland of our country, the minute I got elected the storm clouds on the horizon were getting nearly directly overhead. First, let me make it very clear, poor people aren't necessarily killers. Just because you happen not to be rich doesn't mean you're willing to kill. Presidents, whether things are good or bad, get the blame. I understand that. If this were a dictatorship, it would be a heck of a lot easier, just so long as I'm the dictator.

"Now on the economy, this is clearly a budget. It's got a lot of numbers in it. My plan plays down an unprecedented amount of our national debt. Budget caps were busted, mightily so. And we are reviewing with people like Judd Gregg from New Hampshire and others some budgetary reform measures that will reinstate—you know, possibly reinstate budgetary discipline. But the caps no longer—the caps, I guess they're there. But they didn't mean much.

"More and more of our imports come from overseas. I know how hard it is for you to put food on your families.

"We want our teachers to be trained so they can meet the obligations, their obligations as teachers. We want them to know how to teach the science of reading. In order to make sure there's not this kind of federal— federal cuff link. Reading is the basics for all learning. One of the great things about books is that sometimes there are fantastic pictures. Laura and I really don't realize how bright our children is sometimes until we get an objective analysis. I don't read what's handed to me. As governor of Texas, I have set high standards for our public schools, and I have met those standards. How do you know, if you don't measure, that you have a system that simply suckles kids through. Governor Bush will not stand for the subsidation of failure. Is our children learning?"

I dream of composing a State of the Union address for President Bush by this method. It would probably end with, "My fellow Americans, I want you to know, I know what I believe. I will continue to articulate what I believe and what I believe—I believe what I believe is right. So in conclusion, I believe that hope is in the far distant future, if at all."

THE MISUNDERESTIMATED MAN

by Jacob Weisberg

THE QUESTION I AM MOST FREQUENTLY ASKED about the *Bushisms* series is, "Do you really think the President of the United States is dumb?"

The short answer is yes.

The long answer is yes and no.

Dipping into this volume may leave the impression that George W. Bush is a simple dimwit. Let's face it: a man who cannot talk about education without making a humiliating grammatical mistake ("The illiteracy level of our children are appalling"); who cannot keep straight the three branches of government ("It's the executive branch's job to interpret law"); who coins ridiculous words ("Hispanos," "arbolist," "subliminable," "resignate," "transformationed");

who habitually says the opposite of what he intends ("the death tax is good for people from all walks of life!") sounds like a grade-A, straw-for-brains imbecile.

If you don't care to pursue the matter any further, that view will serve. George W. Bush has governed, for the most part, the way a straightforward numskull of the Right would, undermining the fiscal condition of the nation, squandering the goodwill of the world after September 11, and allowing huge problems (global warming, entitlement spending, AIDS) to metastasize toward catastrophe while botching the major areas of domestic policy through a combination of ideology, incomprehension, and indifference. If Bush isn't exactly the moron he sounds, his synaptic misfirings offer a plausible proxy for the idiocy of his presidency.

In reality, however, there's more to it. The assemblage of a presidential term's worth of malapropisms, solecisms, gaffes, spoonerisms, and truisms—drawn together here from the best of Bushisms old and new—tends to imply that Bush's lack of fluency in English is tantamount to an absence of intelligence. But as we all know from experience, the inarticulate can be shrewd, the fluent fatuous. In Bush's case, the symptoms indicate a specific malady—some kind of language-skill deficit akin to dyslexia—that does not indicate a lack of mental capacity per se. To judge from the President's SAT scores (566 verbal, 640 math), his IQ is somewhere north of average. It's significantly higher than that of any number of politicians respected for their wisdom, such as Bill Bradley (485 verbal).

Bush also compensates with his nonverbal acumen. As he notes, "smart comes in all kinds of different ways." The President's way is an aptitude for connecting to people, in part though his familiar use of nicknames, banter, and physicality. He charms people by remembering who they are and has a powerful memory for details and figures that truly matter to him, such as batting stats from the 1950s. Bush also has a keen political sense, sharpened under the tutelage of Karl Rove.

What's more, calling the President a cretin helps him in various ways. For one, it absolves him of responsibility. Like Reagan, Bush avoids blame for all manner of contradictions, implausible assertions, and outright lies by appearing an amiable dunce. If he knows not what he does, blame goes to the three puppeteers, Cheney, Rove, and Rumsfeld. For another, it breeds sympathy. We wouldn't laugh at FDR because he couldn't walk. Is it less cruel to laugh at GWB because he can't talk? (Perhaps not, but we can't help it.) The soft bigotry of low expectations also means Bush is seen to outperform by merely getting by. Finally, elitist condescension, however merited, helps cement Bush's bond to the public.

But if numskull is an imprecise description of the President, it is not altogether inaccurate. Bush may not have been born stupid, but he has achieved stupidity, and now wears it as a badge of honor. What makes mocking this president fair as well as funny is that Bush is, or at least once was, capable of learning, reading, and thinking. We know he has discipline and can work hard (at least when the goal is reducing his time for a three-mile run). Instead he has chosen, for most of his life, to coast— on name, charm, good looks, and the easy access to capital afforded by family connections. Christopher Hitchens described him perfectly when he commented during the 2000 campaign that Bush was "unusually incurious, abnormally unintelligent, amazingly inarticulate, fantastically uncultured, extraordinarily uneducated, and apparently quite proud of all these things."

The most obvious expression of Bush's choice of ignorance is that, at the age of fifty-seven, he doesn't know anything about policy or history. After years of working as his dad's spear-chucker in Washington, Bush didn't understand the difference between Medicare and Medicaid, the second and third largest federal programs. Well into his plans for invading Iraq, he still couldn't get—despite the frustrated efforts of his briefers—the distinction between Sunni and Shiite Muslims, the key religious divide in a country he was then about to occupy.

Though he sometimes carries books for show, he either does not read them or doesn't absorb anything from them. In one of the Republican primary debates in 2000, Bush was asked what lessons he took from the experience of Dean Acheson and George Marshall, based on an Acheson biography he claimed to be reading. Bush's answer: "The lessons learned are is that the United States must not retreat within our borders. That we must promote the peace. . . . In order promote the peace, I believe we ought to be a free-trading nation." In other words, all Bush got from the book was his own stump—and stumped—speech.

Bush's ignorance is so transparent that many of his intimates do not bother to dispute it even in public. Consider the testimony of several who know him well.

Richard Perle, foreign policy adviser: "The first time I met Bush 43 . . . two things became clear. One, he didn't know very much. The other was that he had the confidence to ask questions that revealed he didn't know very much."

David Frum, former speechwriter: "Bush had a poor memory for facts and figures. . . . Fire a question at him about the specifics of his administration's policies, and he often appeared uncertain. Nobody would ever enroll him in a quiz show."

Laura Bush, spouse: "George is not an overly introspective person. He has good instincts, and he goes with them. He doesn't need to evaluate and reevaluate a decision. He doesn't try to overthink. He likes action."

John DiIulio, former head of faith-based initiatives: "There is no precedent in any modern White House for what is going on in this one: a complete lack of policy apparatus. What you've got is everything—and I mean everything—being run by the political arm. Everything—and I mean everything—is being run by the Mayberry Machiavellis."

Paul O'Neill, former Treasury secretary: "The only way I can describe it is that, well, the President is like a blind man in a roomful of deaf people. There is no discernible connection."

A second, more damning aspect of Bush's mind-set is that he *doesn't want* to know about anything in detail, however important. Since college, he has spilled over with contempt for knowledge, equating learning with snobbery and making a joke of his own anti-intellectualism ("[William F. Buckley] wrote a book at Yale; I read one," he once quipped at a black-tie event.) By Paul O'Neill's account, Bush could sit through an hour-long presentation about the state of the economy without asking a single question. ("I was bored as hell," the President fired back, ostensibly in jest.) Insiders warned O'Neill not to send the President anything longer than two pages—though in the Treasury secretary's experience, Bush read nothing at all.

Closely related to this aggressive ignorance is a third feature of Bush's mentality: laziness. Again, this is a life-long trait. Bush's college grades were mostly C's (including a 73 in Introduction to the American Political System). At the start of the term, one year, the star of the Yale football team spotted him in the back row during the shopping period for courses. "Hey! George Bush is in this class!" Calvin Hill shouted to his teammates. "This is the one for us!" As governor of Texas, Bush would take a long break in the middle of his short workday—for a run followed by a stretch of video golf or computer solitaire. Aides describe a fruit fly's attention span and a policy of zero tolerance for extended discussion.

A fourth and final quality of Bush's mind is that it does not think. The President does not like to hear debates about issues. Offered an option, he makes up his mind quickly and doesn't reconsider. At an elementary school, a child once asked him whether it was hard to make decisions as president. "Most of the decisions come pretty easily for me, to be frank with you," he replied. By leaping to conclusions based on what he "believes," Bush avoids contemplating even the most obvious basic contradictions: between his policy of tax cuts and reducing the deficit; between his call for a humble foreign policy based on alliances and his unilateral assertion of American power; between his support for in-vitro fertilization (which destroys embryos) and his opposition to fetal stem cell research (because it destroys embryos).

Why would someone capable of being smart choose to be stupid? To shed light on that question, it's necessary to examine George W.'s relationship with his father. This filial bond involves more tension than meets the eye. Dad was away for much of his oldest son's childhood—on business trips, in Washington, and abroad. The oldest son grew up closer to his acid-tongued mother, and acted out against the absent parent—through adolescent misbehavior, academic failure, dissipation, and basically not accomplishing anything at all until well into his forties.

Dubya's youthful screwups and smart-aleck attitude reflect some combination of protest, plea for attention, and flailing attempt to compete. Until a decade ago, his résumé read like a send-up of his dad's. Bush senior was a star student at Andover and Phi Beta Kappa at Yale, where he was also captain of the baseball team; Junior struggled through with gentleman's C's and, though he loved baseball, couldn't make the college lineup. *Père* was a bomber pilot in the Pacific; *fils* sat out 'Nam in the Texas Air National Guard, where he lost flying privileges by not showing up. Dad drove to Texas in 1947 to get rich in the oil business and actually did; Son tried the same in 1975 and drilled dry holes for a decade. Bush the elder got elected to Congress in 1966; Shrub ran in 1978, didn't know what he was talking about, and got clobbered.

Through all this incompetent emulation runs an undercurrent of hostility. In an oft-told anecdote circa 1973, GWB—after getting wasted at a party and driving over a neighbor's trash can in Houston—challenged his dad. "I hear you're lookin' for me," W. told the chairman of the Republican National Committee. "You want to go mano a mano right here?" Some years later at a state dinner, he told the Queen of England he was being seated far away because he was the black sheep of the family.

After half a lifetime of this kind of frustration, Bush decided to straighten out and fly right. Nursing a hangover at a fortieth-birthday weekend, he gave up Wild Turkey, cold turkey. Shortly thereafter, with the help of Billy Graham, he put himself in the hands of a higher power and began attending church regularly. He became obsessed with punctuality. He developed a rigid daily routine. Thus did Prince Hal molt into a quasi-evangelical King Henry. And it worked! Putting together a deal to buy the Texas Rangers, the ne'er-do-well finally tasted success. With success, he grew closer to his father, taking on the role of henchboy and family avenger. This culminated in his 1994 challenge to Texas governor Ann Richards, who had twitted the first President Bush at the 1992 Democratic convention ("Poor George can't help it—he was born with a silver foot in his mouth").

Curiously, this late arrival at adulthood did not involve Bush becoming in any way thoughtful. Having originally chosen stupidity as rebellion, he now stuck with it out of conformity. The promise-keeper, reformed alkie path he chose not only drastically curtailed personal choices he no longer wanted, it supplied an all-encompassing order, offered guidance on policy questions, and prevented the need for much in the way of actual information. Bush's old answer to hard questions was "I don't know and who cares." His new answer was "Wait a second while I check with Jesus."

A remaining bit of poignancy in Bush's new life was the unresolved struggle with his father. "All I ask," he implored a reporter while running for governor in 1994, "is that for once you guys stop seeing me as the son of George Bush." In his campaigns, W. has kept his dad offstage (in an exceptional appearance on the eve of the 2000 New Hampshire primary, 41 appeared on stage and called his son "this boy"). While some describe the second Bush presidency as a "restoration," it is in at least equal measure a repudiation of the first. The son's harder-edged conservatism explicitly rejects the old man's approach to such issues as abortion, taxes, and relations with Israel.

This Oedipally induced ignorance has expressed itself most dangerously in Bush's mishandling of the war in Iraq. Dubya polished off his old man's greatest enemy, Saddam Hussein, but only by lampooning 41's great accomplishment at coalition-building in the first Gulf War. Drunk on "moral claret," as Hendrik Hertzberg of *The New Yorker* memorably put it, Bush led the country to war on false pretenses and neglected to plan the occupation that would inevitably follow his invasion. A more knowledgeable and engaged president might have questioned

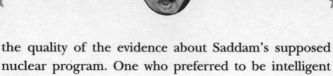

the quality of the evidence about Saddam's supposed nuclear program. One who preferred to be intelligent about what he was getting into surely would have asked about what might happen if the occupiers' reception turned out to be unfriendly. Instead, he got God's sign-off and rolled the dice. Bush's budget-busting tax cuts exemplify a similar phenomenon, driven by an alternate set of ideologues.

As the President says, we misunderestimate him. And we do so at our peril. He was not born stupid; he chose stupidity. This comprehensive edition of *Bushisms* offers a new feature that may be more telling than all the garbled quotes put together—statements by the President that are both clear and grammatically correct, but demonstrably untrue. Bush may look like a well-meaning dolt. On consideration, he's something far more dangerous: a dedicated fool.

1. Who I Am

"I understand reality. If you're asking me as the president, would I understand reality. I do."

–On abortion. Hardball, *May 31, 2000*

"I'm the master of low expectations."

—Aboard Air Force One, June 4, 2003

"I am a person who recognizes the fallacy of humans."

—The Oprah Winfrey Show, September 19, 2000

"I was raised in the West. The west of Texas. It's pretty close to California. In more ways than Washington, D.C., is close to California."

—In Los Angeles, as quoted in the Los Angeles Times, April 8, 2000

"I was a prisoner too—but for bad reasons."

—To Argentine president Nestor Kirchner, on being told that all but one of the Argentine delegates to a summit meeting were imprisoned during the military dictatorship, Monterrey, Mexico, January 13, 2004

"I'm also not very analytical. You know I don't spend a lot of time thinking about myself, about why I do things."

—Aboard Air Force One, June 4, 2003

"I'm not really the type to wander off and sit down and go through deep wrestling with my soul."

–As quoted in Vanity Fair, *October 2000*

"I'm not a very good novelist. But it'd make a pretty interesting novel."

–Austin, Texas, December 5, 2000

"Joe, I don't do nuance."

–To Senator Joseph Biden, as quoted in Time, *February 15, 2004*

"I was not prepared to shoot my eardrum out with a shotgun in order to get a deferment. Nor was I willing to go to Canada. So I chose to better myself by learning how to fly airplanes."

–As quoted in the Houston Chronicle, *May 8, 1994*

"Hell, no. Do you think I'm going to admit that? You are out of your mind. Let me give you the political answer, Mr. Reporter."

–To journalist Skip Hollandsworth, on whether he tried to avoid the draft, Texas Monthly, *May 1994*

"I became totally inebriated with hitting the big one."

–On his oil drilling days, Texas Monthly, *May 1994*

"I understand small business growth. I was one."

–New York Daily News, *February 19, 2000*

"I know something about being a government. And you've got a good one."

–Stumping for Governor Mike Huckabee, Bentonville, Arkansas, November 4, 2002

"I've coined new words, like misunderstanding and Hispanically."

–Radio-Television Correspondents Association dinner, Washington, D.C., March 29, 2001

"The woman who knew that I had dyslexia— I never interviewed her."

–Orange, California, September 15, 2000

"I want everybody to hear loud and clear that I'm going to be the president of everybody."

–Washington, D.C., January 18, 2001

"The most important job is not to be governor, or first lady in my case."

–In Pella, Iowa, as quoted in the San Antonio Express-News, *January 30, 2000*

"I've changed my style somewhat, as you know. I'm less— I pontificate less, although it may be hard to tell it from this show. And I'm more interacting with people."

–Meet the Press, February 13, 2000

"I think the American people—I hope the American—I don't think, let me—I hope the American people trust me."

–*Washington, D.C., December 18, 2002*

"No."

WHOOPS!

—*Response to* Dallas Morning News *reporter Wayne Stater about whether he'd ever been arrested, other than for stealing a Christmas wreath as a college student.*

REALITY CHECK: Bush was also arrested in 1976 for drunken driving while visiting his parents in Kennebunkport, Maine.

"I have been very candid about my past."

–*Press conference, Grand Rapids, Michigan, November 3, 2000*

"I think anybody who doesn't think I'm smart enough to handle the job is underestimating."

–*As quoted in* U.S. News & World Report, *April 3, 2000*

2. What I Believe

"We found the weapons of mass destruction. We found biological laboratories ... we've so far discovered two. And we'll find more weapons as time goes on. But for those who say we haven't found the banned manufacturing devices or banned weapons, they're wrong, we found them."

—*Washington, D.C., May 30, 2003*

REALITY CHECK: President Bush was talking about two trailers found in Iraq that the CIA and Defense Intelligence Agency had concluded were mobile biological weapons labs, despite the lack of any pathogenic residue in either trailer. The CIA and DIA later retracted their claim that the trailers were for WMD. More than nine months after this statement, forces in Iraq still had not found "banned manufacturing devices or banned weapons," and former chief of the Coalition WMD hunt, David Kay, admitted, "We were all wrong, probably."

"I think if you know what you believe, it makes it a lot easier to answer questions. I can't answer your question."

—In response to a question about whether he wished he could take back any of his answers from first debate with Al Gore, Reynoldsburg, Ohio, October 4, 2000

"I know what I believe. I will continue to articulate what I believe and what I believe —I believe what I believe is right."

—Rome, July 22, 2001

"The reason I believe in a large tax cut is because it's what I believe."

—Washington, D.C., December 18, 2000

"I know the human being and fish can coexist peacefully."

—Saginaw, Michigan, September 29, 2000

"It's important for young men and women who look at the Nebraska champs to understand that quality of life is more than just blocking shots."

–Remarks to the University of Nebraska women's volleyball team, the 2001 national champions, Washington, D.C., May 31, 2001

"I also understand how tender the free enterprise system can be."

–White House press conference, Washington, D.C., July 9, 2002

"All in all, it's been a fabulous year for Laura and me."

–Showing a new rug in the Oval Office, December 21, 2001

"I think we agree, the past is over."

–On his meeting with John McCain, quoted in The Dallas Morning News, *May 10, 2000*

"I'm hopeful. I know there is a lot of ambition in Washington, obviously. But I hope the ambitious realize that they are more likely to succeed with success as opposed to failure."

–Interview with the Associated Press, January 18, 2001

"Oftentimes what I try to say in Washington gets filtered and sometimes my words in Washington don't exactly translate directly to the people."

–Kalamazoo, Michigan, March 27, 2001

"America better beware of a candidate who is willing to stretch reality in order to win points."

–Aboard his campaign airplane, September 18, 2000

"Home is important. It's important to have a home."

–Crawford, Texas, February 18, 2001

"And there's no doubt in my mind, not one doubt in my mind, that we will fail."

–Washington, D.C., October 4, 2001

3. Off and Running

"I've got a record not of rhetoric, but a record of results. In my state I led our state to the two biggest tax cuts in the state's history."

—*Des Moines, Iowa, December 13, 1999*

REALITY CHECK: The "two biggest tax cuts" in Texas history were offset by 1997 legislation that implemented a higher sales tax and other new taxes, despite a 1994 campaign promise by Bush to "oppose any legislation establishing a state personal income tax or increasing the sales tax." By 1999, Bush's successor as governor, Rick Perry, was saying that "the tax cut didn't stand the test of time as well as many of us would have liked for it to."

"There's a huge trust. I see it all the time
when people come up to me and say,
'I don't want you to let me down again.'"

–Boston, Massachusetts, October 3, 2000

"There are pledges all the time."

*–On breaking his campaign pledge not to
support a sales tax as governor of Texas,*
This Week with George Stephanopoulos, *January 23, 2000*

"The important question is, how
many hands have I shaked?"

*–Answering a question about why he hadn't spent more time in
New Hampshire,* The New York Times, *October 23, 1999*

"They said, 'You know, this issue doesn't seem to
resignate with the people.' And I said, you know
something? Whether it resignates or not doesn't
matter to me, because I stand for doing what's
the right thing, and what the right thing is
hearing the voices of people who work."

–Portland, Oregon, October 31, 2000

"This is Preservation Month. I appreciate preservation.
It's what you do when you run for president.
You gotta preserve."

*–Speaking at Fairgrounds Elementary School, Nashua,
New Hampshire, during "Perseverance Month,"
quoted in the* Los Angeles Times, *January 28, 2000*

"I do not agree with this notion that somehow if
I go to try to attract votes and to lead people
toward a better tomorrow somehow I get subscribed
to some—some doctrine gets subscribed to me."

–Meet the Press, February 13, 2000

"Really proud of it. A great campaign. And I'm really
pleased with the organization and the thousands
of South Carolinians that worked on my behalf.
And I'm very gracious and humbled."

–To Cokie Roberts, This Week with
George Stephanopoulos, *February 20, 2000*

"I don't think we need to be subliminable about the
differences between our views on prescription drugs."

–Orlando, Florida, September 12, 2000

"It's evolutionary, going from governor to president, and this is a significant step, to be able to vote for yourself on the ballot, and I'll be able to do so next fall, I hope."

—Interview with the Associated Press, March 8, 2000

"Listen, Al Gore is a very tough opponent. He is the incumbent. He represents the incumbency. And a challenger is somebody who generally comes from the pack and wins, if you're going to win. And that's where I'm coming from."

—Detroit, Michigan, September 7, 2000

"The point is, this is a way to help inoculate me about what has come and is coming."

—On his anti-Gore ad, in an interview with The New York Times, *September 2, 2000*

"I think he needs to stand up and say if he thought the president were wrong on policy and issues, he ought to say where."

—Interview with the Associated Press, August 11, 2000

"The fact that he relies on facts—says things that are not factual—are going to undermine his campaign."

—The New York Times, *March 4, 2000*

"As far as the legal hassling and wrangling and posturing in Florida, I would suggest you talk to our team in Florida led by Jim Baker."

—*Crawford, Texas, November 30, 2000*

4. Accidental Wit

"Our budget will run a deficit that will be small and short-term."

WHOOPS!

—*State of the Union Address, January 29, 2002*

REALITY CHECK: The President's 2005 budget, released in February 2004, projected a record deficit of $521 billion.

"They misunderestimated me."

–Bentonville, Arkansas, November 6, 2000

"If there are warning signs on the horizon, we need to pay attention to them."

–Austin, Texas, December 21, 2000

"I recently met with the finance minister of the Palestinian Authority, was very impressed by his grasp of finances."

—Washington, D.C., May 29, 2003

"They have miscalculated me as a leader."

—Westminster, California, September 13, 2000

"Governor, thank you very much. I am here to make an announcement that this Thursday, ticket counters and airplanes will fly out of Ronald Reagan Airport."

—Arlington, Virginia, October 2, 2001

"We want to develop defenses that are capable of defending ourselves and defenses capable of defending others."

—Washington, D.C., March 29, 2001

"Dick Cheney and I do not want this nation to be in a recession. We want anybody who can find work to be able to find work."

—60 Minutes II, *December 5, 2000*

"There's no question that the minute I got elected, the storm clouds on the horizon were getting nearly directly overhead."

–Washington, D.C., May 11, 2001

"One of the common denominators I have found is that expectations rise above that which is expected."

–Los Angeles, California, September 27, 2000

"Never again in the halls of Washington, D.C., do I want to have to make explanations that I can't explain."

–Portland, Oregon, October 31, 2000

"Brie and cheese."

–To reporters, on what he imagines reporters eat, Crawford, Texas, August 23, 2001

"Will the highways on the Internet become more few?"

–Concord, New Hampshire, January 29, 2000

"I hope we get to the bottom of the answer. It's what I'm interested to know."

–As quoted by the Associated Press, April 26, 2000

5. Accidental Wisdom

"I read the report put out by the bureaucracy."

—On an EPA study warning of the dangers of global warming, Washington, D.C., June 4, 2002

REALITY CHECK: At the June 10, 2002, White House press briefing, a reporter noted to Press Secretary Ari Fleischer that President Bush said "he read the report. I believe the report is 260-some pages—he meant he read the full report?" Fleischer responded, "Whenever presidents say they read it, you can read that to be he was briefed." Fleischer then joked that he would get fired for his honesty.

"We ought to make the pie higher."

–South Carolina Republican debate, February 15, 2000

"In my judgment, when the United States says there will be serious consequences, and if there isn't serious consequences, it creates adverse consequences."

–Meet the Press, February 8, 2004

"Oftentimes, we live in a processed world—you know, people focus on the process and not results."

–Washington, D.C., May 29, 2003

"I have said that the sanction regime is like Swiss cheese—that meant that they weren't very effective."

–Washington, D.C., February 22, 2001

"There's an old saying in Tennessee—I know it's in Texas, probably in Tennessee—that says, fool me once, shame on—shame on you. Fool me—you can't get fooled again."

–Nashville, Tennessee, September 17, 2002

We don't believe in planners and deciders making the decisions on behalf of Americans."

–Scranton, Pennsylvania, September 6, 2000

"The senator has got to understand if he's going to have—he can't have it both ways. He can't take the high horse and then claim the low road."

—Florence, South Carolina, February 17, 2000

"I think war is a dangerous place."

—Washington, D.C., May 7, 2003

"If you don't stand for anything, you don't stand for anything. If you don't stand for something, you don't stand for anything."

—Bellevue, Washington, October 31, 2000

"When I was coming up, it was a dangerous world, and you knew exactly who they were. It was us versus them, and it was clear who them was. Today, we are not so sure who the they are, but we know they're there."

—Iowa Western Community College, January 21, 2000

"This is still a dangerous world. It's a world of madmen and uncertainty and potential mental losses."

—At a South Carolina oyster roast, January 14, 2000

"Actually, I—this may sound a little West Texan to you, but I like it. When I'm talking about—when I'm talking about myself, and when he's talking about myself, all of us are talking about me."

–Hardball, *May 31, 2000*

"First, let me make it very clear, poor people aren't necessarily killers. Just because you happen to be not rich doesn't mean you're willing to kill."

–*Washington, D.C., May 19, 2003*

"Over the long term, the most effective way to conserve energy is by using energy more efficiently."

–*Radio address, May 12, 2001*

"It's very important for folks to understand that when there's more trade, there's more commerce."

–*Quebec City, Canada, April 21, 2001*

"I'm sure you can imagine it's an unimaginable honor to live here."

–*In a White House address to agriculture leaders, June 18, 2001*

"Well, I think if you say you're going to do something and don't do it, that's trustworthiness."

—CNN online chat, August 30, 2000

"There's no such thing as legacies. At least, there is a legacy, but I'll never see it."

—To Catholic leaders at the White House, January 31, 2001

6. Presidential Education

"Our SAT scores have improved since I've been the governor. You need to get your researchers to do a better job."

—*To Steve Forbes, Republican primary presidential debate in Manchester, New Hampshire, January 26, 2000*

REALITY CHECK: In 1994, Bush's first year in office as governor of Texas, the mean SAT I score in Texas among "college-bound seniors" was 990, while the national average was 1003. In 1999, the mean SAT I score in Texas had increased by 3 to 993, while the national average had increased by 13, to 1016. So, relative to the rest of the country, Texas's SAT scores actually decreased.

"There is book smart and the kind of smart
that helps do calculus. But smart is also instinct
and judgment and common sense.
Smart comes in all kinds of different ways."

—CNN, September 19, 2000

"And if you're interested in the quality of education
and you're paying attention to what you hear at Laclede
[Elementary School], why don't you volunteer?
Why don't you mentor a child how to read?"

—St. Louis, Missouri, January 5, 2004

"As governor of Texas, I have set high standards for
our public schools, and I have met those standards."

—CNN online chat, August 30, 2000

"Reading is the basics for all learning."

*—Announcing his "Reading First" initiative in Reston, Virginia,
March 28, 2000*

"I read the newspaper."

*—In answer to a question about his reading habits,
New Hampshire Republican debate, December 2, 1999*

"I glance at the headlines just to kind of get a flavor for what's moving. I rarely read the stories, and get briefed by people who are probably read the news themselves."

–Washington, D.C., September 21, 2003

"You know, sometimes when you study history,
you get stuck in the past."

*–Recounting what he told Russian president Vladimir Putin,
in an interview with Peggy Noonan,*
The Wall Street Journal, *June 25, 2001*

"One of the great things about books is sometimes
there are some fantastic pictures."

–U.S. News & World Report, January 3, 2000

"I want to thank the astronauts who are with us, the
courageous spacial entrepreneurs who set such a
wonderful example for the young of our country."

–Washington, D.C., January 14, 2004

"Rarely is the question asked: Is our children learning?"

–Florence, South Carolina, January 11, 2000

"You teach a child to read, and he or her will
be able to pass a literacy test."

–Townsend, Tennessee, February 21, 2001

"[T]he illiteracy level of our children are appalling."
—*Washington, D.C., January 23, 2004*

"We must have the attitude that every child
in America—regardless of where they're raised
or how they're born—can learn."
—*New Britain, Connecticut, April 18, 2001*

"We want our teachers to be trained so they can
meet the obligations, their obligations as teachers.
We want them to know how to teach the science of
reading. In order to make sure there's not this
kind of federal—federal cuff link."
—*Fritsche Middle School, Milwaukee, Wisconsin, March 30, 2000*

"I love the idea of a school in which people come to get
educated and stay in the state in which they're educated."
—*Waco, Texas, August 13, 2002*

"*Columbia* carried in its payroll classroom experiments
from some of our students in America."
—*Bethesda, Maryland, February 3, 2003*

"I know there's a lot of young ladies who are growing up wondering whether or not they can be champs. And they see the championship teams from USC and University of Portland here, girls who worked hard to get to where they are, and they're wondering about the example they're setting. What is life choices about?"

–Washington, D.C., February 24, 2003

"I don't have to accept their tenants. I was trying to convince those college students to accept my tenants. And I reject any labeling me because I happened to go to the university."

*–On his visit to Bob Jones University, Today,
February 23, 2000*

"I want it to be said that the Bush administration was a results-oriented administration, because I believe the results of focusing our attention and energy on teaching children to read and having an education system that's responsive to the child and to the parents, as opposed to mired in a system that refuses to change, will make America what we want it to be—a literate country and a hopefuller country."

–Washington, D.C., January 11, 2001

7. The Economy, Stupid

**"Two and a half years ago, we in-
herited an economy in recession."**

—*Miami, Florida, June 30, 2003*

REALITY CHECK: In November 2001, a report by the nonpartisan National Bureau of Economic Research concluded the recession began in March 2001, two months after the start of Bush's first term. Bush himself acknowledged this in a radio address in December 2001, saying "This week, the official announcement came that our economy has been in recession since March. And, unfortunately, to a lot of Americans, that news comes as no surprise." A few months later, he began claiming that the recession began while Clinton was still president.

31

"See, without the tax relief package, there would have been a deficit, but there wouldn't have been the commiserate—not commiserate—the kick to our economy that occurred as a result of the tax relief."

—Washington, D.C., December 15, 2000

"Didn't we already give them a break at the top?"

—To economic advisers urging the elimination of taxes on dividends, as quoted by Paul O'Neill, Washington, D.C., November 26, 2002

"It is not Reaganesque to support a tax plan that is Clinton in nature."

—Los Angeles, February 23, 2000

"The government is not the surplus's money, Vice President."

—The Washington Post, November 5, 2000

"It's your money. You paid for it."

—La Crosse, Wisconsin, October 18, 2000

"A tax cut is really one of the anecdotes to coming out of an economic illness."

–The Edge with Paula Zahn, *September 18, 2000*

"I'm confident we can work with Congress to come up with an economic stimulus package that will send a clear signal to the risk takers and capital formators of our country."

–*Washington, D.C., September 17, 2001*

WHOOPS!

"This growth and jobs package is essential in the short run. It's an immediate boost to the economy. And these proposals will help stimulate investment and put more people back to work, is what we want to have happen. They are essential for the long run, as well—to lay the groundwork for future growth and future prosperity. That growth will bring the added benefit of higher revenues for the government—revenues that will keep tax rates low, while fulfilling key obligations and protecting programs such as Medicare and Social Security."

—*Chicago, Illinois, January 7, 2003*

REALITY CHECK: From the 2003 *Economic Report of the President:* "The modest effect of government debt on interest rates does not mean that tax cuts pay for themselves with higher output. Although the economy grows in response to tax reductions (because of higher consumption in the short run and improved incentives in the long run), it is unlikely to grow so much that lost tax revenue is completely recovered by the higher level of economic activity."

"If the terriers and bariffs are torn down,
this economy will grow."

–Rochester, New York, January 7, 2000

WHOOPS!

"If you look at the appropriations bills that were passed under my watch, in the last year of President Clinton, discretionary spending was up 15 percent, and ours have steadily declined."

—Meet the Press, *February 8, 2004*

REALITY CHECK: According to Bush's Office of Management and Budget, discretionary spending increased 31 percent during Bush's first three years in office. It rose only 3 percent in Clinton's final year.

"Governor Bush will not stand for
the subsidation of failure."

–*Florence, South Carolina, January 11, 2000*

"Ann and I will carry out this equivocal message
to the world: markets must be open."

–*Swearing-in ceremony for Secretary of Agriculture Ann Veneman,
Washington, D.C., March 2, 2001*

"My plan reduces the national debt, and fast. So fast, in fact, that economists worry that we're going to run out of debt to retire."

—*Radio address, February 24, 2001*

REALITY CHECK: Not a problem, as it turned out. In January 2004, the International Monetary Fund released a study expressing concern that the "United States is on course to increase its net external liabilities to around 40 percent of GDP within the next few years—an unprecedented level of external debt for a large industrial country."

"I've always found the best investments are those that you salt away based on economics."

—*Austin, Texas, January 4, 2001*

"My pan plays down an unprecedented amount of our national debt."

—*Budget address to Congress, February 27, 2001*

8. Hostile Environment

WHOOPS!

"You've got to ask the question, is the air cleaner since I became governor, and the answer is yes."

—*Austin, Texas, May 20, 1999*

REALITY CHECK: The Environmental Protection Agency reported a 10 percent increase in industrial emissions in Texas between 1994 and 1997. Smog had reached such high levels in Dallas that the federal government threatened to withdraw millions of dollars of highway funds in 1999. A *Washington Post* article pointed out that in 1999 Texas ranked first in toxic air release, ozone components, airborne carcinogens, and number of days with unhealthy ozone. Twenty-seven of the country's thirty highest ozone readings that year occurred in Texas.

"Just remember it's the birds that's supposed
to suffer, not the hunter."

*–Advising quail hunter and New Mexico senator Pete Domenici,
Roswell, New Mexico, January 22, 2004*

"Arbolist . . . Look up the word. I don't know,
maybe I made it up. Anyway, it's an arbo-tree-ist,
somebody who knows about trees."

–As quoted in USA Today, *August 21, 2001*

"John Thune has got a common-sense vision for good forest policy. I look forward to working with him in the United Nations Senate to preserve these national heritages."

—*South Bend, Indiana, October 31, 2002*

"There are some monuments where the land is so widespread, they just encompass as much as possible. And the integral part of the—the precious part, so to speak—I guess all land is precious, but the part that the people uniformly would not want to spoil, will not be despoiled. But there are parts of the monument lands where we can explore without affecting the overall environment."

—*Media round table, Washington, D.C., March 13, 2001*

"It's good to see so many friends here in the Rose Garden. This is our first event in this beautiful spot, and it's appropriate we talk about policy that will affect people's lives in a positive way in such a beautiful, beautiful part of our national—really, our national park system, my guess is you would want to call it."

—*Washington, D.C., February 8, 2001*

"My administration is committed to a leadership role on the issue of climate change."

—*Washington, D.C., June 11, 2001*

REALITY CHECK: The Bush administration still has not issued a counterproposal to the rejected Kyoto Protocol, nor have any of his environmental policies addressed the rising level of carbon emissions, thought to be a major cause of global warming.

"It would be helpful if we opened up ANWR [the Arctic National Wildlife Refuge]. I think it's a mistake not to. And I would urge you all to travel up there and take a look at it, and you can make the determination as to how beautiful that country is."

–*Washington, D.C., March 29, 2001*

9. A Leader of Great Energy

WHOOPS!

"The idea of placing caps on CO_2 does not make economic sense for America."

—*Washington, D.C., March 29, 2001*

REALITY CHECK: On July 1, 2003, *The Washington Post* revealed that for months the EPA had withheld findings that showed a Senate antipollution plan that included caps on carbon emissions was only marginally more expensive then Bush's Clear Skies initiative, which shunned such caps.

"It is clear our nation is reliant upon big foreign oil. More and more of our imports come from overseas."

—*Beaverton, Oregon, September 25, 2000*

"Natural gas is hemispheric. I like to call it hemispheric in nature because it is a product that we can find in our neighborhoods."

–Austin, Texas, December 20, 2000

"The California crunch really is the result of not enough power-generating plants and then not enough power to power the power of generating plants."

–Interview with The New York Times, *January 14, 2001*

"We need an energy bill that encourages consumption."

–Trenton, New Jersey, September 23, 2002

WHOOPS!

"The SEC fully investigated the stock deal. . . . I was exonerated."

—*As quoted in the* Houston Chronicle, *October 1994, on a 1992–1993 SEC investigation into possible insider trading by George W. Bush as an executive board member of Harken Oil*

REALITY CHECK: When the SEC concluded its investigation into Bush's dealings in October 1993, its associate director of enforcement warned that its investigation into Bush's dealings "must in no way be construed as indicating that the party has been exonerated or that no action may ultimately result."

"And we need a full affront on an energy crisis that
is real in California and looms for other parts of
our country if we don't move quickly."

–*Washington, D.C., March 29, 2001*

"There was no malfeance involved. This was an honest
disagreement about accounting procedures. . . . There
was no malfeance, no attempt to hide anything."

–*Defending his actions while at Harken Energy,*
Washington, D.C., July 8, 2002

10. Leader of the Free World

WHOOPS!

"At the time I wanted to fight, yes, and I was willing to train for whatever experience came my way. I actually tried, I tried for what's called a 'palace alert' program from my guard program to transfer on a temporary basis for assignments, and I was too junior to get the assignments."

—*About his joining the Air National Guard,* The Boston Globe, *March 28, 1999*

REALITY CHECK: According to David Corn's book *The Lies of George W. Bush,* "When Bush entered the Guard, he had to say on his application papers whether he was willing to volunteer for overseas duty. He checked the box that read 'do not volunteer.'"

"For diplomacy to be effective, words must be credible, and no one can now doubt the word of America."

—State of the Union Address, January 20, 2004

"This foreign policy stuff is a little frustrating."

—As quoted in the New York Daily News, *April 23, 2002*

"We had a good Cabinet meeting, talked about a lot of issues. Secretary of State and Defense brought us up-to-date about our desires to spread freedom and peace around the world."

—Washington, D.C., August 1, 2003

"Security is the essential roadblock to achieving the road map to peace."

—Washington, D.C., July 25, 2003

"I think it's very important for world leaders to understand that when a new administration comes in, the new administration will be running the foreign policy."

—Interview with USA Today, *January 12, 2001*

"Redefining the role of the United States from enablers to keep the peace to enablers to keep the peace from peacekeepers is going to be an assignment."

–Interview with The New York Times, *January 14, 2001*

"This is a world that is much more uncertain than the past. In the past we were certain, we were certain it was us versus the Russians in the past. We were certain, and therefore we had huge nuclear arsenals aimed at each other to keep the peace. That's what we were certain of. . . . You see, even though it's an uncertain world, we're certain of some things. We're certain that even though the 'evil empire' may have passed, evil still remains. We're certain there are people that can't stand what America stands for. . . . We're certain there are madmen in this world, and there's terror, and there's missiles and I'm certain of this, too: I'm certain to maintain the peace, we better have a military of high morale, and I'm certain that under this administration, morale in the military is dangerously low."

–Albuquerque, New Mexico, May 31, 2000

"First, we would not accept a treaty that would not have been ratified, nor a treaty that I thought made sense for the country."

–On the Kyoto accord, in an interview with
The Washington Post, *April 24, 2001*

"My administration has been calling upon all the leaders in the—in the Middle East to do everything they can to stop the violence, to tell the different parties involved that peace will never happen."

–Crawford, Texas, August, 13, 2001

"There's a lot of people in the Middle East who are desirous to get into the Mitchell process. And—but first things first. The—these terrorist acts and, you know, the responses have got to end in order for us to get the framework—the groundwork —not framework, the groundwork to discuss a framework for peace, to lay the—all right."

–Referring to former senator George Mitchell's report on Middle East peace, Crawford, Texas, August 13, 2001

"I don't want nations feeling like that they can bully ourselves and our allies. I want to have a ballistic defense system so that we can make the world more peaceful, and at the same time I want to reduce our own nuclear capacities to the level commiserate with keeping the peace."

—Des Moines, Iowa, October 23, 2000

"We cannot let terrorists and rogue nations hold this nation hostile or hold our allies hostile."

—Des Moines, Iowa, August 21, 2000

"[T]he best way to find these terrorists who hide in holes is to get people coming forth to describe the location of the hole, is to give clues and data."

—Washington, D.C., December 15, 2003

"And, yes, we're always interested in dealing with people who have harmed American citizens."

—Washington, D.C., February 25, 2002

"America's first temptation is withdrawal, to build a proud tower of protectionism and isolation. In a world that depends on America to reconcile old rivals and balance ancient ambitions, this is the shortcut to chaos."

—At the Ronald Reagan Presidential Library, Simi Valley, California, November 19, 1999

"My administration is promoting free and fair trade, to open up new markets for America's entrepreneurs and manufacturers and farmers, and to create jobs for America's workers."

—State of the Union Address, January 20, 2004

REALITY CHECK: In 2002, President Bush ordered extensive tariffs on imported steel, eliciting threats of retaliatory tariffs from other countries and protests from disparate free-market supporters. In November 2003, the World Trade Organization ruled that the tariffs were illegal, clearing the way for sanctions if Bush didn't repeal them. Additionally, in September 2003, WTO talks about liberalizing trade with poorer nations broke down in Cancún when the Bush administration (and other developed countries) refused to cut farming subsidies.

11. Grecians, Kosovians, and Other Foreigners

WHOOPS!

"The British government has learned that Saddam Hussein recently sought significant quantities of uranium from Africa."

—*State of the Union Address, January 28, 2003*

REALITY CHECK: In October 2002, George Tenet insisted that President Bush not use this British intelligence about Saddam Hussein seeking uranium from Niger ("Africa") in his October 7 speech in Cincinnati because the CIA had discovered that it was false. However, Bush included it in his 2003 State of the Union Address. On July 7, 2003, the administration sheepishly backtracked: "Knowing all that we know now, the reference to Iraq's attempt to acquire uranium from Africa should not have been included in the State of the Union speech."

"Iran would be dangerous if they
have a nuclear weapon."

—Washington, D.C., June 18, 2003

"General . . . I can't name the general."

*—When asked to name the President of Pakistan,
Boston, Massachusetts, November 3, 1999*

"I've got very good relations with President Mubarak
and Crown Prince Abdallah and the
King of Jordan, Gulf Coast countries."

—Washington, D.C., May 29, 2003

"What I'm suggesting to you is, if you can't name the
foreign minister of Mexico, therefore, you know,
you're not capable of what you do. But the truth of
the matter is you are, whether you can or not."

—As quoted in the Seattle Post-Intelligencer, *November 6, 1999*

"For a century and a half now, America and Japan
have formed one of the great and enduring
alliances of modern times."

—Tokyo, Japan, February 18, 2002

"The United States and Russia are in the midst
of a transformationed relationship that will
yield peace and progress."

—Washington, D.C., November 13, 2001

"Russia is no longer our enemy and therefore we
shouldn't be locked into a Cold War mentality that says
we keep the peace by blowing each other up. In my
attitude, that's old, that's tired, that's stale."

—Des Moines, Iowa, June 8, 2001

"But I also made it clear to [Vladimir Putin] that
it's important to think beyond the old days of
when we had the concept that if we blew each
other up, the world would be safe."

—Washington, D.C., May 1, 2001

"You saw the president yesterday. I thought he
was very forward leaning, as they say in
diplomatic nuanced circles."

*—Referring to his meeting with Russian president Vladimir Putin,
Rome, July 23, 2001*

"There's nothing more deep than recognizing Israel's right to exist. That's the most deep thought of all. . . . I can't think of anything more deep than that right."

–Washington, D.C., March 13, 2002

"I understand that the unrest in the Middle East creates unrest throughout the region."

–Washington, D.C., March 13, 2002

"Keep good relations with the Grecians."

–As quoted in The Economist, *June 12, 1999*

"Kosovians can move back in."

–Inside Politics, April 9, 1999

"If the East Timorians decide to revolt, I'm sure I'll have a statement."

–Quoted by Maureen Dowd, The New York Times, *June 16, 1999*

"Whatever it took to help Taiwan defend theirself."

–On how far we'd be willing to go to defend Taiwan, Good Morning America, *April 25, 2001*

"We spent a lot of time talking about Africa, as we should. Africa is a nation that suffers from incredible disease."

–Gothenburg, Sweden, June 14, 2001

"It's about past seven in the evening here so we're actually in different time lines."

–Congratulating newly elected Philippine president Gloria Macapagal Arroyo, Washington, D.C., January 2001

"Neither in French nor in English nor in Mexican."

–Declining to answer reporters' questions at the Summit of the Americas, Quebec City, Canada, April 21, 2001

12. Bring 'Em On

"He's a threat because he deals with Al Qaeda."

—*On Saddam Hussein,*
November 7, 2002

REALITY CHECK: According to *The New York Times,* Al Qaeda officials in custody told CIA interrogators that Osama bin Laden had rejected entreaties from some of his lieutenants to work with Saddam Hussein. According to intelligence sources cited by David Ignatius in the November 28, 2003, edition of *The Washington Post,* "Prior to the war, the CIA and Britain agreed that despite contact between Saddam and Al Qaeda over the years, there had been no substantive, institutional cooperation. Nothing we have learned in recent months would cause us to change that view."

"My answer is bring them on."

—On Iraqi militants attacking U.S. forces,
Washington, D.C., July 3, 2003

"We do know that Saddam Hussein had the intent
and the capabilities to cause great harm. We know
he was a great danger. . . . What we don't know yet
is what we thought and what the Iraqi Survey
Group has found, and we want to look at that."

—Washington, D.C., February 2, 2004

"When I was a kid I remember that they used to
put out there in the Old West a wanted poster.
It said, Wanted: Dead or Alive."

—Washington, D.C., September 18, 2001

"President Musharraf, he's still tight with us on the
war against terror, and that's what I appreciate.
He's a—he understands that we've got to keep
Al Qaeda on the run, and that by keeping him on
the run, it's more likely we will bring him to justice."

—Ruch, Oregon, August 22, 2002

"But the true threats to stability and peace are these nations that are not very transparent, that hide behind the—that don't let people in to take a look and see what they're up to. They're very kind of authoritarian regimes. The true threat is whether or not one of these people decide, peak of anger, try to hold us hostage, ourselves; the Israelis, for example, to whom we'll defend, offer our defenses; the South Koreans."

–Media roundtable, Washington, D.C., March 13, 2001

"The war on terror involves Saddam Hussein because of the nature of Saddam Hussein, the history of Saddam Hussein, and his willingness to terrorize himself."

–Grand Rapids, Michigan, January 29, 2002

"I was proud the other day when both Republicans and Democrats stood with me in the Rose Garden to announce their support for a clear statement of purpose: you disarm, or we will."

–Speaking about Saddam Hussein, Manchester, New Hampshire, October 5, 2002

"Iraq has made several attempts to buy high-strength aluminum tubes used to enrich uranium for a nuclear weapon."

—*Speech to the United Nations, September 12, 2002*

"Our intelligence sources tell us that he has attempted to purchase high-strength aluminum tubes suitable for nuclear weapons production."

—*State of the Union Address, January 28, 2003*

REALITY CHECK: Three weeks before Bush's State of the Union speech, the International Atomic Energy Agency had reported that the tubes were "consistent" with manufacturing requirements for ordinary artillery and "not directly suitable" for uranium enrichment. It has since been confirmed that the tubes were for nonnuclear munitions.

"There's no doubt in my mind that we should allow the world worst leaders to hold America hostage, to threaten our peace, to threaten our friends and allies with the world's worst weapons."

–*South Bend, Indiana, September 5, 2002*

"The suicide bombings have increased. There's too many of them."

–*Albuquerque, New Mexico, August 15, 2001*

WHOOPS!

"I would remind you that when the inspectors went into Iraq and were denied, finally denied access [in 1998], a report came out of the Atomic—the IAEA, that they were six months away from developing a weapon. I don't know what more evidence we need."

—*Camp David, Maryland, September 7, 2002*

REALITY CHECK: What the IAEA actually said was, "There are no indications that Iraq has achieved its program's goal of producing nuclear weapons" and "there are no indications of Iraq having retained any physical capability for the indigenous production of weapon–usable nuclear material in amounts of any practical significance." The report also noted that there was no "indication that Iraq has otherwise acquired such material."

"We've got hundreds of sites to exploit, looking for the chemical and biological weapons that we know Saddam Hussein had prior to our entrance into Iraq."

–*Santa Clara, California, May 2, 2003*

"These people don't have tanks. They don't have ships. They hide in caves. They send suiciders out."

–*Speaking about terrorists, Portsmouth, New Hampshire, November 1, 2002*

WHOOPS!

"The United Nations concluded in 1999 that Saddam Hussein had biological weapons sufficient to produce over 25,000 liters of anthrax—enough doses to kill several million people. He hasn't accounted for that material. He's given no evidence that he has destroyed it."

—*State of the Union Address, January 28, 2003*

REALITY CHECK: The American and British forces now controlling Iraq have found no evidence that Saddam had any anthrax.

WHOOPS!

"The United Nations concluded that Saddam Hussein had materials sufficient to produce more than 38,000 liters of botulinum toxin—enough to subject millions of people to death by respiratory failure. He hadn't accounted for that material. He's given no evidence that he has destroyed it."

—*State of the Union Address, January 28, 2003*

REALITY CHECK: The American and British forces now controlling Iraq have found no evidence that Saddam had any botulinum toxin.

"We ended the rule of one of history's worst tyrants, and in so doing, we not only freed the American people, we made our own people more secure."

—Crawford, Texas, May 3, 2003

"There is no such thing necessarily in a dictatorial regime of iron-clad absolutely solid evidence. The evidence I had was the best possible evidence that he had a weapon."

—Meet the Press, February 8, 2004

WHOOPS!

"Our intelligence officials estimate that Saddam Hussein had the materials to produce as much as 500 tons of sarin, mustard, and VX nerve agent. In such quantities, these chemical agents could also kill untold thousands. He's not accounted for these materials. He has given no evidence that he has destroyed them."

—State of the Union Address, January 28, 2003

REALITY CHECK: American and British forces now controlling Iraq have found no evidence that Saddam had any of the materials that could be used to create sarin, mustard gas, or VX nerve agent.

"I urge the leaders in Europe and around the world to take swift, decisive action against terror groups such as Hamas, to cut off their funding, and to support—cut funding and support, as the United States has done."

—Washington, D.C., June 25, 2003

"After all, a week ago, there were—Yasser Arafat was boarded up in his building in Ramallah, a building full of evidently German peace protesters and all kinds of people. They're now out. He's now free to show leadership, to lead the world."

—Washington, D.C., May 2, 2002

13. Bad for Your Health

"As a result of private research, more than sixty genetically diverse stem cell lines already exist."

—*Televised address from the Oval Office, Washington, D.C., August 9, 2001*

REALITY CHECK: In the speech: President Bush indicated that there were already sixty stem cell lines ready to be used for research. Many scientists doubted this claim and, on May 22, 2003, the chief of the federal National Institute of Health admitted, "NIH support has helped increase to eleven the number of human embryonic stem cell lines that are widely available for all researchers."

"It would be a mistake for the United States Senate to allow any kind of human cloning to come out of that chamber."

–Washington, D.C., April 10, 2002

"We're concerned about AIDS inside our White House—make no mistake about it."

–Washington, D.C., February 7, 2001

"If I'm the president, we're going to have emergency-room care, we're going to have gag orders."

–Saint Louis, Missouri, October 18, 2000

WHOOPS! **"The direct cost of liability insurance and the indirect cost from unnecessary medical procedures raise the federal government's health care costs by at least $28 billion a year."**

—*Little Rock, Arkansas, January 26, 2004*

REALITY CHECK: According to a 2004 study by the Congressional Budget Office, there is "no evidence that restrictions on tort liability reduce medical spending."

"Drug therapies are replacing a lot of medicines
as we used to know it."

–Saint Louis, Missouri, October 18, 2000

14. Death, Taxes, and Death Taxes

"The deficit would have been bigger without the tax relief package."

—*Washington, D.C., November 13, 2002*

REALITY CHECK: According to the Congressional Budget Office, the first Bush tax cut made a substantial contribution to the deficit.

"For every fatal shooting, there were roughly three nonfatal shootings. And, folks, this is unacceptable in America. It's just unacceptable. And we're going to do something about it."

–*Philadelphia, Pennsylvania, May 14, 2001*

"The only things that I can tell you is that every case I have reviewed I have been comfortable with the innocence or guilt of the person that I've looked at. I do not believe we've put a guilty . . . I mean innocent person to death in the state of Texas."

—National Public Radio, June 16, 2000

"I want to thank you for taking time out of your day to come and witness my hanging."

—At the dedication of his portrait, Austin, Texas, January 4, 2002

"We need to counter the shock wave of the evildoer by having individual rate cuts accelerated and by thinking about tax rebates."

—Washington, D.C., October 4, 2001

"Not over my dead body will they raise your taxes."

—Ontario, California, January 5, 2002

"States should have the right to enact reasonable laws and restrictions particularly to end the inhumane practice of ending a life that otherwise could live."

—Cleveland, Ohio, June 29, 2000

WHOOPS! "You know, when I was one time campaigning in Chicago, a reporter said, 'Would you ever have a deficit?' I said, 'I can't imagine it, but there would be one if we had a war, or a national emergency, or a recession.' Never did I dream we'd get the trifecta."

—*Houston, Texas, June 14, 2002*

REALITY CHECK: There is no record of Bush saying anything of the sort. In July 2002, the *Chicago Tribune* reported, "Some senior advisers have asked Bush to eliminate the [trifecta story] from the stump speech. They hope the move will quash the talk among Washington critics that Bush may be telling tall tales."

"Those of us who spent time in the agricultural sector and in the heartland, we understand how unfair the death penalty is."

–*Omaha, Nebraska, February 28, 2001*

"I talked about making the death tax permanent so that Rolf can pass his assets from—to a family member if he so chooses."

–*After meeting with small-business owners, O'Fallon, Missouri, March 18, 2002*

"I firmly believe the death tax is good for people from all walks of life all throughout our society."

—Waco, Texas, August 13, 2002

WHOOPS!

"My jobs and growth plan would reduce tax rates for everyone who pays income tax."

—Weekly presidential radio address, April 26, 2003

REALITY CHECK: An Urban Policy Institute–Brookings Institution study revealed that 8.1 million tax filers would not receive any tax cuts from Bush's 2003 tax cut proposal. Additionally, a Republican spokesperson for the House Ways and Means Committee confirmed that many middle- and lower-income families would not receive an expansion in the child-care tax credit.

15. Race to the Bottom

"Pickering has got a very strong record on civil rights."

*—On Federal judiciary nominee
Charles Pickering at a press conference,
March 13, 2002*

REALITY CHECK: Pickering switched from the Democratic party to the Republican party in 1964 after a Democratic Congress passed the landmark Civil Rights Act. Pickering announced his switch by using the coded language of segregationists: "The people of our state were heaped with humiliation and embarrassment at the Democratic Convention. And this has convinced me beyond a doubt that Mississippians do not now and will not in the future have any useful place in the national Democratic Party." Many Pickering supporters claim that he was a hero for standing up to the Ku Klux Klan. A 1967 statement that Pickering signed condemned the Klan by saying: "While we believe in continuing our southern way of life and realize that outside agitators have caused much turmoil and racial hatred, let there be no misunderstanding, we oppose such activities, but law and order must prevail." "Southern way of life" was the commonly used euphemism for segregation. In 1994, Pickering, then a judge, called up a friend in the Justice Department seeking help in reducing the sentence of a convicted cross burner, eliciting complaints from legal ethicists.

"It's very interesting when you think about it, the slaves who left here to go to America, because of their steadfast and their religion and their belief in freedom, helped change America."

–Dakar, Senegal, July 8, 2003

"Do you have blacks, too?"

–To Brazilian president Fernando Cardoso, Washington, D.C., November 8, 2001

"Over 75 percent of white Americans own their home, and less than 50 percent of Hispanos and African Americans don't own their home. And that's a gap, that's a home ownership gap. And we've got to do something about it."

–Cleveland, Ohio, July 1, 2002

"The Senate needs to leave enough money in the proposed budget to not only reduce all marginal rates but to eliminate the death tax, so that people who build up assets are able to transfer them from one generation to the next, regardless of a person's race."

—*Washington, D.C., April 5, 2001*

"A lot of times in the rhetoric, people forget the facts. And the facts are that thousands of small businesses— Hispanically owned or otherwise—pay taxes at the highest marginal rate."

—*To the Hispanic Chamber of Commerce, Washington, D.C., March 19, 2001*

"The Bob Jones policy on interracial dating, I mean I spoke out on interracial dating. I spoke against that. I spoke out against interracial dating. I support the policy of interracial dating."

—CBS News, *February 25, 2000*

"If affirmative action means what I just described, what I'm for, then I'm for it."

—*Saint Louis, Missouri, October 18, 2000*

"What I am against is quotas. I am against hard quotas, quotas they basically delineate based upon whatever. However they delineate, quotas, I think, vulcanize society. So I don't know how that fits into what everybody else is saying, their relative positions, but that's my position."

–*Quoted by Molly Ivins,* San Francisco Chronicle, *January 21, 2000*

"Quotas are bad for America. It's not the way America is all about."

–*Saint Louis, Missouri, October 18, 2000*

"Whether you're here by birth, or whether you're in America by choice, you contribute to the vitality of our life. And for that, we are grateful."

–*Washington, D.C., May 17, 2002*

"If he's—the inferences is that somehow he thinks slavery is a—is a noble institution—I would—I would strongly reject that assumption. That John Ashcroft is an open-minded, inclusive person."

–*Interview with Tom Brokaw,* NBC Nightly News with Tom Brokaw, *January 15, 2001*

16. Friends and Foes

"I got to know Ken Lay when he was the head of the—what they call the Governor's Business Council in Texas. He was a supporter of Ann Richards in my run in 1994. And she had named him the head of the Governor's Business Council. And I decided to leave him in place, just for the sake of continuity. And that's when I first got to know Ken and worked with Ken."

—*Washington, D.C., January 10, 2002*

REALITY CHECK: Bush met the former Enron CEO in 1989 when Lay chaired a campaign to locate Bush's father's library in Houston. In 2001, Lay told *The Dallas Morning News* that in 1989 he had spent "quality time" with Bush. During Bush's 1994 gubernatorial run, Lay contributed $37,500 to the Bush campaign—about three times as much as he contributed to Bush's opponent, Ann Richards. According to the *Houston Chronicle,* an October 2000 video circulated among Enron employees filmed Lay saying about Bush that "I strongly supported Bush when he ran for governor of Texas both times."

"You believe in the Almighty, and I believe in the Almighty. That's why we'll be great partners."

—To Turkish Prime Minister Recap Tayyip Erdogan, Washington, D.C., December 10, 2002

"I confirmed to the prime minister that we appreciate our friendship."

—After meeting with Prime Minister Jean Chrétien of Canada, February 5, 2001

"We both use Colgate toothpaste."

—On Tony Blair, Camp David, Maryland, February 23, 2001

"I must confess. It did confuse some of the folks at the Crawford, Texas, coffee shop when I was traveling around the country with Theodore Kennedy."

—Chicago, Illinois, May 13, 2002

"I looked the man in the eye. I found him to be very straightforward and trustworthy. . . . I was able to get a sense of his soul."

–After meeting with Russian President Vladimir Putin, June 16, 2001

"She's just trying to make sure Anthony gets a good meal—Antonio."

–On Laura Bush inviting U.S. Supreme Court justice Antonin Scalia to dinner at the White House, NBC Nightly News with Tom Brokaw, *January 14, 2001*

"Laura and I are proud to call John and Michelle Engler our friends. I know you're proud to call him governor. What a good man the Englers are."

–Grand Rapids, Michigan, November 3, 2000

"He married, like me, above his head."

–On U.S. ambassador to Canada Paul Cellucci, Quebec City, April 22, 2001

"Bill wrote a book at Yale. I read one."

–On William F. Buckley, Al Smith dinner, New York City, October 19, 2000

"I'm also honored to be here with the Speaker of the House—just happens to be from the state of Illinois. I'd like to describe the Speaker as a trustworthy man."

—Chicago, Illinois, March 6, 2001

"And, most importantly, Alma Powell, secretary of Colin Powell, is with us."

—Washington, D.C., January 30, 2003

"I do remain confident in Linda. She'll make a fine labor secretary. From what I've read in the press accounts, she's perfectly qualified."

—Defending Secretary of Labor nominee Linda Chavez, Austin, Texas, January 8, 2001

"I haven't had a chance to talk, but I'm confident we'll get a bill that I can live with if we don't."

—Referring to the McCain-Kennedy patients' bill of rights, Brussels, Belgium, June 13, 2001

17. In the Name of Love

"By helping to build an Afghanistan that is free from this evil and is a better place in which to live, we are working in the best traditions of George Marshall."

—Lexington, Virginia, April 21, 2002

REALITY CHECK: President Bush was referring to the Marshall Plan, under which the United States helped fund the rebuilding of Europe after World War II. The President included no money for Afghan peacekeepers in his 2003 budget. Nor did the White House originally propose any money for USAID (the chief federal humanitarian aid agency) to spend in Afghanistan, despite requests for $200 million. After much criticism, the Bush administration relented and allocated $100 million.

"The true strength of America happens when a neighbor loves a neighbor just like they'd like to be loved themselves."

—Elizabeth, New Jersey, June 16, 2003

"People say, how can I help on this war against terror? How can I fight evil? You can do so by mentoring a child, by going into a shut-in's house and say I love you."

—Washington, D.C., September 19, 2002

"God loves you, and I love you. And you can count on both of us as a powerful message that people who wonder about their future can hear."

—Los Angeles, California, March 3, 2004

"We'll be a great country where the fabrics are made up of groups and loving centers."

—Kalamazoo, Michigan, March 27, 2001

"We must all hear the universal call to like your neighbor just like you like to be liked yourself."

—Financial Times, January 14, 2000

WHOOPS!

"I ask the Congress to commit $15 billion over the next five years, including nearly $10 billion in new money, to turn the tide against AIDS in the most afflicted nations of Africa and the Caribbean."

—*State of the Union Address, January 28, 2003*

REALITY CHECK: Only $8.5 billion dollars was new money; the rest had been previously allocated for other AIDS-related programs. $6.8 billion of that $8.5 billion will not be available until 2006, despite the underfunding of most of the major global AIDS organizations. As cited in *The Book on Bush*, by Eric Alterman and Mark J. Green.

"We can come together to heal whatever wounds may exist, whatever residuals there may be."

–*Washington, D.C., December 18, 2000*

"It's negative to think about blowing each other up. That's not a positive thought. That's a Cold War thought. That's a thought when people were enemies with each other."

–*Interview with Peggy Noonan,* The Wall Street Journal, *June 25, 2001*

"There's only one person who hugs the mothers and the widows, the wives and the kids upon the death of their loved one. Others hug, but having committed the troops, I've got an additional responsibility to hug and that's me and I know what it's like."

–Washington, D.C., December 11, 2002

18. A Faith-Based Presidency

"These good works deserve our praise. They deserve the assistance of the federal government."

—*On Americorps, State of the Union Address, Washington, D.C., January 29, 2002*

WHOOPS!

REALITY CHECK: President Bush has not asked Congress for any new Americorps funding. On June 17, 2003, a press release from Senator John McCain pointed out that without additional funding, "the corporation will be forced to cut its volunteer force to a mere 2,036 members, meaning that many states will see their competitive grants drop by as much as 90 percent."

"Our priorities is our faith."

—*Greensboro, North Carolina, October 10, 2000*

"I don't bring God into my life to—to, you know, kind of be a political person."

—Interview with Tom Brokaw aboard Air Force One, April 24, 2003

"We've got pockets of persistent poverty in our society, which I refuse to declare defeat—I mean, I refuse to allow them to continue on. And so one of the things that we're trying to do is to encourage a faith-based initiative to spread its wings all across America, to be able to capture this great compassionate spirit."

—O'Fallon, Missouri, March 18, 2002

"The federal government and the state government must not fear programs who change lives, but must welcome those faith-based programs for the embetterment of mankind."

—Stockton, California, August 23, 2002

"My pro-life position is I believe there's life. It's not necessarily based in religion. I think there's a life there, therefore the notion of life, liberty, and pursuit of happiness."

—As quoted in the San Francisco Chronicle, *January 23, 2001*

"Justice was being delivered to a man who defied that gift from the Almighty to the people of Iraq."

–On Saddam Hussein, Washington, D.C., December 15, 2003

"Major combat operations in Iraq have ended. In the battle of Iraq, the United States and our allies have prevailed."

—May 1, 2003, on the deck of the USS Abraham Lincoln, under a banner saying "Mission Accomplished."

"President Bush Announces Combat Operations in Iraq Have Ended."

—Headline on the White House Web site above May 1 speech

REALITY CHECK: On August 14, 2003, Bush said, "We still have combat operations going on. . . . It's a different kind of combat mission, but, nevertheless, it's combat, just ask the kids that are over there killing and being shot at." On February 1, 2004, the coalition military fatality count had reached 623 soldiers. The vast majority—452 of them—occurred after President Bush delivered this speech. On July 17, 2003, CENTCOM Commander General John Ábizaid said the Coalition was stuck in a "classical guerilla war."

"Anyway, after we go out and work our hearts out, after you go out and help us turn out the vote, after we've convinced the good Americans to vote, and while they're at it, pull that old George W. lever, if I'm the one, when I put my hand on the Bible, when I put my hand on the Bible, that day when they swear us in, when I put my hand on the Bible, I will swear to not—to uphold the laws of the land."

—Toledo, Ohio, October 27, 2000

"We have practically banished religious values and religious institutions from the public square and constructed a 'discountfort zone' for even discussing our faith in public settings."

—Milwaukee, Wisconsin, September 9, 2000

"So on behalf of a well-oiled unit of people who came together to serve something greater than themselves, congratulations."

—Remarks to the University of Nebraska women's volleyball team, the 2001 national champions, Washington, D.C., May 31, 2001

19. Family Values

WHOOPS!

"We must reduce the role and scope of the federal government, returning it to the limited role our forefathers envisioned when they wrote the tenth amendment to the Constitution, giving the states all power not specifically granted to the federal government."

—*As quoted in* The Washington Post Magazine, *September 19, 1999*

REALITY CHECK: On January 20, 2004, President Bush proposed a constitutional amendment to prevent states from legalizing gay marriage.

"I thought how proud I am to be standing up beside my dad. Never did it occur to me that he would become the gist for cartoonists."

–Newsweek, *February 28, 2000*

"Now, we talked to Joan Hanover. She and her husband, George, were visiting with us. They are near retirement—retiring—in the process of retiring, meaning they're very smart, active, capable people who are retirement age and are retiring."

–*Alexandria, Virginia, February 12, 2003*

"Families is where our nation finds hope, where wings take dream."

–*La Crosse, Wisconsin, October 18, 2000*

"I know how hard it is for you to put food on your family."

–*To the Chamber of Commerce, Greater Nashua, New Hampshire, January 27, 2000*

"The best way to relieve families from time is to let them keep some of their own money."

–Westminster, California, September 13, 2000

"It's important for us to explain to our nation that life is important. It's not only life of babies, but it's life of children living in, you know, the dark dungeons of the Internet."

–Arlington Heights, Illinois, October 24, 2000

"Maybe she'll be able to join us in Florida. If not, she can clean out her room."

–On the recovery of his daughter Jenna from an appendectomy, December 26, 2000

"I think we ought to raise the age at which juveniles can have a gun."

–Saint Louis, Missouri, October 18, 2000

"In other words, I don't think people ought
to be compelled to make the decision which
they think is best for their family."

–Washington, D.C., December 11, 2002

"So thank you for reminding me about the importance
of being a good mom and a great volunteer as well."

–Saint Louis, Missouri, January 5, 2004

"Laura and I really don't realize how bright our children
is sometimes until we get an objective analysis."

–To Tim Russert, CNBC, April 15, 2000

"The way I like to put it is this. There's no bigger
issue for the President to remind the moms and
dads of America, if you happen to have a child,
be fortunate to have a child."

–Washington, D.C., March 7, 2001

GOV. BUSH: It just seems so un-American to me, the picture of the guy storming the house with a scared little boy [Elián Gonzalez] there. I talked to my little brother, Jeb—I haven't told this to many people. But he's the governor of—I shouldn't call him my little brother— my brother, Jeb, the great governor of Texas.

JIM LEHRER: Florida.

GOV. BUSH: Florida. The state of the Florida.

–The NewsHour with Jim Lehrer, *April 27, 2000*

"I do think we need for a troop to be able to house his family. That's an important part of building morale in the military."

–*Tyndall Air Force Base, Florida, March 12, 2001*

20. Civic Lessons

"We must uncover every detail and learn every lesson of September 11."

WHOOPS!

—*While signing a bill that created an independent 9/11 investigative commission, November 27, 2002*

REALITY CHECK: A January 31, 2004, article in *The Washington Post* reported that "The White House, already embroiled in a public fight over the deadline for an independent commission's investigation of the September 11, 2001, attacks, is refusing to give the panel notes on presidential briefing papers taken by some of its own members, officials said this week. The standoff has prompted the ten-member commission to consider issuing subpoenas for the notes and has further soured relations between the Bush administration and the bipartisan panel, according to sources familiar with the issue. Lack of access to the materials would mean that the information they contain could not be included in a final report about the attacks, several officials said."

"[T]hat's just the nature of democracy. Sometimes pure politics enters into the rhetoric."

—Crawford, Texas, August 8, 2003

"If this were a dictatorship, it would be a heck of a lot easier, just so long as I'm the dictator."

—Washington, D.C., December 18, 2002

"[A]s you know, these are open forums. You're able to come and listen to what I have to say."

—Washington, D.C., October 28, 2003

"I am mindful of the difference between the executive branch and the legislative branch. I assured all four of these leaders that I know the difference, and that difference is they pass the laws and I execute them."

—Washington, D.C., December 18, 2000

"The legislature's job is to write law. It's the executive branch's job to interpret law."

–Austin, Texas, November 22, 2000

"And so, in my State of the—my State of the Union—or state—my speech to the nation, whatever you want to call it, speech to the nation—I asked Americans to give four thousand years—four thousand hours over the next—the rest of your life—of service to America. That's what I asked—four thousand hours."

–Bridgeport, Connecticut, April 9, 2002

"I suspect that had my dad not been president, he'd be asking the same questions: How'd your meeting go with so-and-so? . . . How did you feel when you stood up in front of the people for the State of the Union Address— state of the budget address, whatever you call it."

–Interview with The Washington Post, *March 9, 2001*

"I am mindful not only of preserving executive powers for myself but for predecessors as well."

–Washington, D.C., January 29, 2001

"I also have picked a secretary for Housing and Human Development. Mel Martinez from the state of Florida."

—Austin, Texas, December 20, 2000

"Presidents, whether things are good or bad, get the blame. I understand that."

—Washington, D.C., May 11, 2001

"I need to be able to move the right people to the right place at the right time to protect you, and I'm not going to accept a lousy bill out of the United Nations Senate."

–*South Bend, Indiana, October 31, 2002*

"I want each and every American to know for certain that I'm responsible for the decisions I make and each of you are as well."

–Live with Regis, *September 20, 2000*

"The administration I'll bring is a group of men and women who are focused on what's best for America, honest men and women, decent men and women, women who will see service to our country as a great privilege and who will not stain the house."

–*Des Moines, Iowa, January 15, 2000*

21. America the Beautiful

"**The American economy depends on fairness and honesty. The vast majority of businesses uphold those values. With this law, we have new tools to enforce those values, and we will use those tools aggressively to defend our free enterprise system against corruption and crime.**"

—On the Sarbanes-Oxley Act, July 30, 2002

REALITY CHECK: Sarbanes-Oxley called for a $338 million increase in the SEC budget. However, in mid-October 2002, the Bush administration's budget revealed that it would only increase the SEC budget by $130 million, less than 40 percent of the amount prescribed by Congress.

"Our country puts $1 billion a year up to help feed the hungry. And we're by far the most generous nation in the world when it comes to that, and I'm proud to report that. This isn't a contest of who's the most generous. I'm just telling you as an aside. We're generous. We shouldn't be bragging about it. But we are. We're very generous."

—*Washington, D.C., July 16, 2003*

"I can't tell you what it's like to be in Europe, for example, to be talking about the greatness of America. But the true greatness of America are the people."

—*Visiting the Jefferson Memorial, Washington, D.C., July 2, 2001*

"I want you to know that farmers are not going to be secondary thoughts to a Bush administration. They will be in the forethought of our thinking."

—*Salinas, California, August 10, 2000*

"They didn't think we were a nation that could conceivably sacrifice for something greater than our self; that we were soft, that we were so self-absorbed and so materialistic that we wouldn't defend anything we believed in. My, were they wrong. They just were reading the wrong magazine or watching the wrong Springer show."

—*Washington, D.C., March 12, 2002*

"The folks who conducted to act on our country on September 11 made a big mistake. They underestimated America. They underestimated our resolve, our determination, our love for freedom. They misunderestimated the fact that we love a neighbor in need. They misunderestimated the compassion of our country. I think they misunderestimated the will and determination of the commander in chief, too."

–Langley, Virginia, September 26, 2001

"Well, it's an unimaginable honor to be the president during the Fourth of July of this country. It means what these words say, for starters. The great inalienable rights of our country. We're blessed with such values in America. And I—it's—I'm a proud man to be the nation based upon such wonderful values."

–Visiting the Jefferson Memorial, Washington, D.C., July 2, 2001

"I think we're making progress. We understand
where the power of this country lay. It lays in the
hearts and souls of Americans. It must lay in our
pocketbooks. It lays in the willingness for people
to work hard. But as importantly, it lays in the fact
that we've got citizens from all walks of life, all
political parties, that are willing to say, I want to
love my neighbor. I want to make somebody's life
just a little bit better."

–Concord Middle School, Concord, North Carolina, April 11, 2001

"I'm thrilled to be here in the breadbasket of America
because it gives me a chance to remind our fellow
citizens that we have an advantage here in
America—we can feed ourselves."

–Stockton, California, August 23, 2002

"Any time we've got any kind of inkling that somebody is thinking about doing something to an American and something to our homeland, you've just got to know we're moving on it, to protect the United Nations Constitution, and at the same time, we're protecting you."

—Aberdeen, South Dakota, October 31, 2002

"We've had a great weekend here in the Land of the Enchanted."

—Albuquerque, New Mexico, May 12, 2003
(New Mexico's state nickname is "Land of Enchantment.")

"You're free. And freedom is beautiful. And, you know, it'll take time to restore chaos and order—order out of chaos. But we will."

—Washington, D.C., April 13, 2003

"There may be some tough times here in America. But this country has gone through tough times before, and we're going to do it again."

—Waco, Texas, August 13, 2002

ACKNOWLEDGMENTS

As Bushisms has grown into a cottage industry, I've lost the ability to run it on my own. David Newman of Yale Law School scours the transcripts and runs down the rumors for me on an ongoing basis. David also helped frame and organize the material included in this book. Slate's uberintern Avi Zenilman pulled together the fact-checking modules on a tight deadline. Goofy images of our commander in chief have been supplied with astonishing efficiency and creativity, for all four Bushisms books, by ace photo researcher Toby Greenberg. I'm also grateful to Jeff Posternack of the Wylie Agency and to Bruce Nichols, the editor of this series, who took the idea and ran with it from the get-go. Thanks finally to the alert readers of Slate and to my colleagues, who found the majority of these gems laying (or lying) in plain sight.